My Cousins Explained

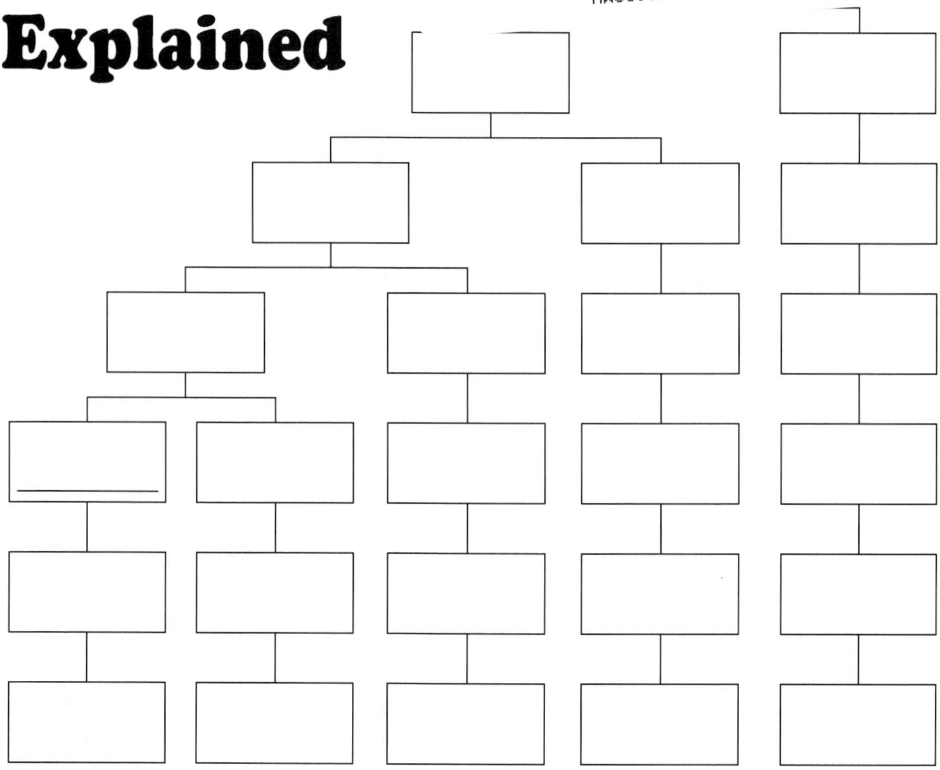

This journal belongs to:..

Made in the USA
Middletown, DE
01 December 2021

53964483R00068